Contents

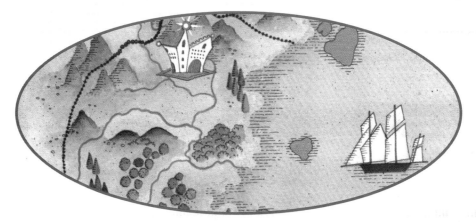

In a Galaxy Far, Far Away

by Mark Cotta Vaz

From *The Complete Star Wars Trilogy Scrapbook*

The lights in the theatre go down. An image of another world appears on screen. It looks completely real, but it's not. It's the world created for the *Star Wars* movies, the most successful movie series of all time.

In this world Luke Skywalker, Han Solo, Obi-Wan Kenobi, Princess Leia and the droids C-3P0 and R2-D2 fight to bring peace back to their galaxy. Check out some of the amazing places they go.

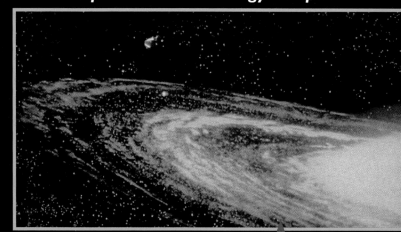

In the *Star Wars* galaxy, star formations spin like wheels in space.

Obi-Wan Kenobi and Luke Skywalker both live on the desert planet called Tatooine.

A space pod enters the Tatooine atmosphere. On board are droids C-3P0 and R2-D2 with a message for Obi-Wan Kenobi from Princess Leia.

There are many ways to travel on Tatooine. Sail barges move across the desert using sails to catch the wind. Anti-gravity units keep the barges off the ground.

Landspeeders are another anti-gravity vehicle. Here Luke, Obi-Wan and the droids pilot their landspeeder into the city of Mos Eisley.

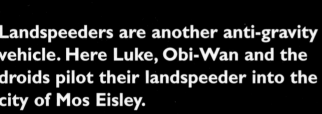

This is Obi-Wan Kenobi's house in the Dune Sea.

The remote star system of Endor, above the planet Endor, includes a moon full of forests. In the great trees live the furry little beings called Ewoks. The Ewok villages are built around the tree trunks. Wooden bridges and walkways connect the forest community.

Photos: COURTESY OF LUCASFILM LTD.

Bringing Ideas to Life

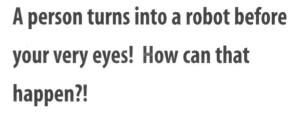

A person turns into a robot before your very eyes! How can that happen?!

It's not real, of course. It's a special effect created by a computer artist. Computer artists use their imagination to bring amazing effects to life.

*C*omputer artist Ellen Poon works for Industrial Light and Magic. With her computer, she can do just about anything. But how does she come up with her effects?

"First I read the script," she explains. "I look at the storyboards drawn by artists who work with the director. The storyboards are drawings that show what is supposed to happen in each frame. The director might have suggested a special effect for a scene. It's my job to create it."

Ellen says that it can take her weeks to come up with the right effect. She gets her ideas from cartoons, movies, books — anything that crosses her path. "Sometimes ideas come to me quickly," she says. "I might wake up in the middle of the night and think, 'Hey! That's what I'm going to do.'"

When it's time to create the special effect, Ellen turns to her computer. She has to match the effect to the movement of the actor. With the scene from the movie on her computer screen, she uses the computer to draw the effect over the scene. Then she works on making it move the way it should. Later she works with a team to add light and colour. When everything looks right, it's all put together.

Being a computer artist is a lot of work. "It helps to have a sense of humour," Ellen says. "A big part of what animators do is make people laugh. So it's a good idea if you learn to laugh too."

Becoming a Computer Artist

How do you get to be a computer artist? Learning lots of math and science is a good start. According to Ellen Poon, "It's impossible to make objects on a computer move without understanding math. And you can't make a cartoon bird fly unless you know what makes real birds fly."

— Fran Buncombe

Cartoon College

Canada has some of the best schools in the world for computer animation. And there are so many talented animators in Canada that Disney has opened studios in both Vancouver and Toronto.

One Toronto artist has turned her own company into a school. Maxine Schacker's studio is called Max the Mutt Animation Inc. It makes the cartoon "The Jazz Bears Jamboree."

In 1997, Maxine and her partner Tina Seemann started giving classes at their studio. The classical animation school is called Studio M. The students there learn things like acting, life drawing, storyboarding and animation. All the teachers are artists or animators, so the students are learning from experts.

Especially talented students sometimes work on "At the Jazz Bears Jamboree." As Maxine says, "We give them real studio experience without all the pressure."

— Barry Brown

Maxine Schacke (left) and Tina Seemann, partn in Max the Mut Animation Inc.

Photo and stills: Disney /Photofest

Ric Sluiter working on *Mulan*

Drawing a Dream

According to Chinese legend, Mulan was a girl with a dream. She would have a great future. Her own courage made her dream come true. Most Disney movies tell stories of dreams that come true — like *Mulan*.

Sometimes dreams come true for the people who work on those movies too. Ric Sluiter is one of those people. He always wanted to be an animation artist. He went to Sheridan College in Toronto to learn animation. Disney liked the drawings he sent them, and they called him.

Today Ric is the art director of *Mulan*. But putting the movie together hasn't been easy. Preparations began in 1994. Artists working on the movie spent hours visiting ancient caves in China, where they sketched artwork from the time of Mulan. Back at the studio, Ric's job was to direct a team of 400 artists. "Anything that wasn't exactly right was redone," he says. "Even an eyelash."

If your dream is going to come true, it should be perfect!

Blast Off!

Photograph by Walter Wick
Riddle by Jean Marzollo

I spy two funnels, a flashlight, a cart,
An ice-cream scoop, a magnet, and START;

Write an "I Spy" Riddle
Try to spy all the way-out objects named in this riddle. When you're done, write your own "I Spy" riddle about other objects in the photo.

Six safety pins, a man on the run,
A plane, and the numbers from ten to one.

SUPER HEROES

By Elaine Scott

Comic books take readers out of the real world into a world where fantastic things happen — funny things, adventurous things, amazing things. Chances are your parents and grandparents had stacks of comic books when they were young. Perhaps you have a stack of your own right now.

The First Comic Books

Comic books began in 1911, when the popular Mutt and Jeff strips were gathered into book form and published. However, it was another 22 years before the comic book as we know it really got started.

In 1932, two high school students became interested in a kind of writing called science fiction. Jerry Siegel and Joe Shuster decided to put out their own magazine. They produced it by using their school's mimeograph machine. Jerry wrote stories about a super hero who could "hurdle skyscrapers, leap one-eighth of a mile into the air, lift tremendous weights, run faster than a train . . . and nothing less than a bursting shell could penetrate his skin!" Joe illustrated the character doing all of these things — and more. Jerry and Joe called their stories "The Reign of the Supermen." They had created a legend.

Action Comics

DC Comics published the first issue of "Detective Comics" in March, 1937. In June, 1938 they decided to introduce another comic book, to be called "Action Comics." They also bought the rights to the Superman character. The rest, as people say, is history. The Superman stories took the country by storm, and other comics soon followed with more superheroes.

Superman first appeared in a comic book in 1938. By 1940, there were 60 new comic books on the newsstands. By 1941, there were 108 more. These featured heroes with names such as Batman, Captain Marvel, Wonder Woman, Sub-Mariner, Flash Gordon and Buck Rogers.

Funny Comics

The main purpose of the comics has always been entertainment. New comic books began to appear that made readers laugh. Many of the characters in these comic books were already famous from movie cartoons. Others appeared for the first time in comic books. Later they became "stars" in movie theatres and on television. Mickey Mouse and Donald Duck were already popular when they appeared in comic book form. But Archie Andrews and his friends Jughead, Veronica, Reggie and Betty were created as comic book characters. They had their own animated television show much later.

Comic Book Fans

Comic book readers take their comics seriously. In 1992, DC Comics announced that Superman would be killed at the hands of a character named Doomsday. The news caused a great deal of comment in newspapers and on television. On October 4, 1992, the *New York Times* ran an editorial commenting on the Man of Steel's death. The writer ended the piece by noting, "Doubtlessly, DC Comics will see to it that Superman is born again. He's too big a part of the business to stay dead." Finally, in 1993, the one and only Superman returned, 55 years after his comic book debut.

The Canadian Connection

Superman may be an American hero, but he's got roots in Canada. Creator Joe Shuster was born in Toronto and lived there until he was 10. Every day after school, his father would read him the comics from *The Daily Star*. Shuster loved the comics and the newspaper that ran them. So he started working as a newsboy selling *The Daily Star*. For the first two years of the Superman cartoon, the newspaper that Clark Kent worked for was called *The Daily Star*.

Idea Man

One of the most amazing figures in the world of comic books isn't a super hero — he's Stan Lee. Stan started out writing comic books as a teenager. In 1940, he joined Marvel Comics. In 1962, he co-created The Amazing Spider-Man. Stan is still with Marvel Comics today. He writes the daily Spider-Man strip, although others write the comic book adventures.

Stan has given life to other super heroes as well. These include the Incredible Hulk, Iron Man, the Fantastic Four and the original X-Men. Where does he get so many ideas? He says the best places are the plays of William Shakespeare, legends and myths, and authors like Mark Twain, Edgar Allan Poe and Sir Arthur Conan Doyle, creator of Sherlock Holmes.

Louise Profeit-LeBlanc
Storyteller

by Susan Petersiel Berg

Louise Profeit-LeBlanc is of the Nacho N'yak Dun nation, or Big River People. Inspired by her peoples' traditions, she has been telling stories all her life.

Photo: John Hatch

Questions for Louise Profeit-LeBlanc

What does it mean to be a storyteller?

It means that you tell a story without a book. The stories I tell are in my heart and in my head. Kids are surprised when they hear me say that we have three ears — two on the sides of our head and one in our heart. You listen to the stories with your heart, and then you tell them.

What made you want to be a storyteller?

I saw a need because so many young people have moved to the city and don't have grandparents to tell stories to them. Also, I met storyteller Angela Sydney, who became my friend and mentor. She hoped someone would carry on her stories, and I felt responsible to do that for her. I want to share our traditional knowledge with children. I want them to know the stories and history and wisdom that come from people living in this part of the world.

How do you come up with your stories?

Most have been passed on to me by elders — not only my own grandmother, but all of the grandmothers I've come to know. Before I use a story I've heard, I ask the original teller if it's OK.

What were the first stories you heard?

They were stories told in Northern Tutchone, the Athabaskan language. The adults would be telling them to one

another and I was probably sleeping in my hammock. Later on my grandmother would tell them to me in English.

Photo: Bruce Barrett

PROFILE

Name:
Louise Profeit-LeBlanc

Occupation:
Storyteller and Native heritage adviser for the Yukon government

Home:
Whitehorse, Yukon

Favourite Book:
Anything by Margaret Atwood

Favourite Storytellers:
Susan Klassen, Itah Sadu and mentor Angela Sydney

First Storytelling Experience:
At age five, sharing with my classmates stories my grandmother had taught me

What did you learn from your storyteller grandmother?

That there are lessons everywhere. We could be out trapping and she'd tell a story of another little girl out trapping. Cues for stories are everywhere in the environment. And stories are an easy way to teach kids lessons. Elders wouldn't say you were lying about something. They would tell you a story about someone who lied. Grandma was tricky like that.

Should storytellers record their stories on paper?

I think so. Some tellers don't want to have their stories writte down. But I'm afraid if we don record them they'll be lost. The grandchildren of today's tellers will never hear their stories. Three Yukon storytellers — Kit Smith, Rachel Dawson and Angela Sydney — have agreed to have their stories written dov word for word.

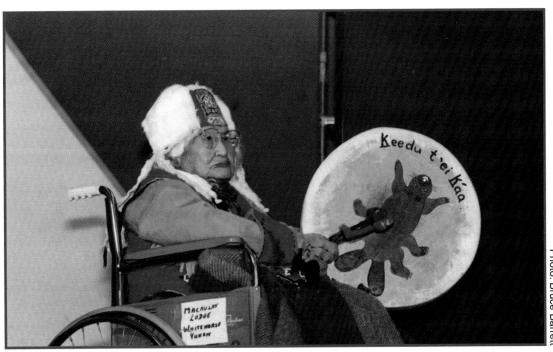

Photo: Bruce Barrett

What do you like best about being a storyteller?

I like the connection between the storyteller and the story. There's a spirit that moves in while I'm telling. Sometimes I tell stories and hardly remember doing it. It's the spirit of my ancestors. That's the part I like best.

Tips for Telling a Good Story

1. Have a reason for telling a story — to share good news, make somebody laugh, help somebody learn something.

2. Remember to have a beginning, a middle and an end to your story.

3. Respect your audience. All audience members are equal.

Boy Soup

written and illustrated by Loris Lesynski

Giant woke up with a big hurting head.
"I am sore, I am sick, I feel awful," he said.
Groaning, he shovelled his blankets aside
and reached for his *Giants' Home Medical Guide*.

With sofa-sized fingers, he leafed through the book,
and in between sneezes so loud that he shook,
he found all his symptoms, page seventy-one:
   "Queasiness, wheeziness, coughing begun.
   Completely depleted, and tending to droop."
   The only prescription?
      A bowl of Boy Soup.

"Can't *be*," said the giant. "Would be a disgrace."
But a big greedy grin spread all over his face.
"Of course, if I'm ill, that's a decent excuse.
And think of the broth a good boy could produce.
   One *buttery* boy — or better, a group!
   A half-dozen lads would make wonderful soup!"

Catching the boys was as easy as pie:
he stretched down his thick giant arm through the sky
and rested his hand at the top of a tree
where children were playing. They just didn't see
the branch they were grabbing could grab *them*.
    Too late!
That's how the giant got five boys — and Kate.

"Why *should* I feel guilty?" the giant began,
when six angry children protested his plan.
"It's here in this authorized medical book!"
Kate asked, "Before supper, could I have a look?"

She read every word in the faded ink
and said, "May I have just a minute to think?"
Kate racked her brain at a furious rate
to save all her friends from this hideous fate.
The giant was ready. Oh, *how* could they flee?
    Their ten rubber running shoes — *that* was the key!

Just as the giant came closer to scoop
the lads for his horrid medicinal soup,
Kate gave a signal, the tiniest look.
The boys understood. They leapt to the book
and started a dance, half a shuffle, half-run,
and jogged back and forth on page seventy-one.
    Up the page, down the page, sidestep, repeat,
    'til most of each word was erased by their feet.

"Now I can't check it!" the giant complained.
But Kate said, "I've read it, I'll gladly explain.
    The book said quite clearly — of this I am sure —
    Boy Soup is soup *made by* boys, that is the cure."

"But . . ." sniffed the giant, "I thought boys went *in* it.
I think I'm confused . . . can you give me a minute?"

"Oh, no," Kate proclaimed,
"you're too sick, don't you know.
We have to work fast. Come on, fellows, let's go!"

The boys cooked the carrots, the boys boiled the peas,
then seasoned the soup with a handful of fleas.
They put in some mud and some thick yellow glue
and a generous dollop of dandruff shampoo.

Kate poured in pepper and red hot sauce,
rotten bananas and candy floss,
sour green pickles and beans in the can
        — all simmered together as part of the plan.

The giant tipped the whole potful of soup down his throat
    sat back
    and *sighed*
'til he started to bloat,
and the pepper, the mud and the pickles combined.

The giant let out a most terrible whine —
and SPIT out the soup with so mighty a blast
that it blew
    all the children
        down homeward
            at last!

Puppet Magic

by Sara Lee Lewis

The theatre is dark. Everyone is quiet. Suddenly, puppets seem to glow on stage. That's the magic of black-light theatre. Right now, it's on stages around the world, thanks to the Mermaid Theatre of Nova Scotia.

The play, called *Borrowed Black*, is based on a book by Ellen Bryan Obed. The actors wear black body suits and face stockings. They work under ultra-violet light. Their costumes and the puppets they operate are painted with a paint that glows in the dark.

Together, actors and puppets tell the fantasy story of a creature who creates his body by borrowing parts from nature. One day he goes too far. He borrows the moon, leaving the whole world dark. When he drops the moon, it shatters and he buries it. Not until many years later is it found and returned to the sky.

Mermaid Theatre's Jim Morrow with some of his puppet friends. "We all loved *Borrowed Black*," Jim says. "And it's a way for us to promote Canadian literature."

*The Little Lame Prince —
the King and Courtiers in
the court yard*

Mermaid Theatre has created a wide range of puppet plays over the past 25 years. The group's purpose is to share with children the wonders of the imagination. They also want to share Canadian talent with the rest of the world.

No matter what the play, Mermaid's puppets are always amazing. They range from the tiny people of Lilliput in *Gulliver's Travels* to Nova Scotia giant Anna Swan.

And the puppeteers don't hide behind their puppets. They are right on stage with them. "If you've got an actor hiding behind a stage, it raises questions. Who is it? Who's down there?" explains Jim Morrow, one of Mermaid's directors.

Take a look at some of the worlds Mermaid Theatre has created.

*Borrowed Black —
The fisher people
looking at Borrowed
Black's shack*

The Little Lame Prince — Older telling part of his tale

Borrowed Black — Borrowed Black with his sack of wind and Mousey Mate

Photos: Courtesy of Mermaid Theatre of Nova Scotia

Kids On Screen

By Linda McAvoy

It's not easy to pretend to be someone from a totally different time period — or from another universe. Ask any actor! Read how these young Canadian screen stars feel about playing someone from a world very different from their own.

Other Times, Other Places

Thirteen-year-old Michael Caloz is from Montreal. He's been to both the future and the past. In the science fiction movie *Screamers*, the year was 2078. Michael played David, who battled humans on a frozen, far-off planet called Sirius 6B. In the feature film *Little Men*, he played Nat. That story took place in Boston in 1871.

Reading the script and the original book, *Little Men* by Louisa May Alcott, helped Michael to feel he was in a different time. "The costumes helped me too, because they were so different from clothes we wear today. I had to wear old-fashioned long johns, laced-up boots, a vest, buttoned shirts and even a long nightgown to sleep in."

Michael likes roles that are a change from normal, everyday parts. "They're fun — they challenge me because I can't rely on skills I'm used to."

Photo: Courtesy of Oscars/Abrams/Zinel

Michael Calo

Everything Old

Martha MacIssac and Jessica Pellerin have been spending a lot of time in the past as well. As actors in the television series "Emily of New Moon," the two act the parts of children who lived almost a century ago. The show, which is filmed on location in Prince Edward Island, uses lots of old-fashioned costumes and props — everything from pinafores to chamber pots.

Martha, 14, plays the lead role of Emily. Jessica plays her best friend Ilse. One thing they both notice is that people's speech was different back then. "There are some words, like 'neat' and 'cool,' that you can't say because they just weren't used. Or they had a different meaning." But after playing their characters for so long, they find a few old-fashioned words from the scripts creeping into their everyday speech.

The show's costumes are familiar to them now too. "At first it was really neat to dress up in different clothes from a hundred years ago," says Martha. "But now it just seems normal."

Jessica Pellerin (left) and Martha MacIssac

Photo: Courtesy of Salter Street Films, from the television series "Emily of New Moon," a co-production of Slater Street Films and Cinar Films

Who Was That Masked Kid?

Fourteen-year-old Kevin Zegers is spending his time in Australia these days. He's pretending to be scared of a computerized lizard in a movie called Komodo. "This is a hard movie to shoot," he says. "I have to make it look like I'm terrified. I'm also acting in front of a blue screen so they can add special effects later. It's a lot of pretending, but I'm finding it easier as I get older and more experienced." This is the first time he's played the part of someone who lived long ago.

Kevin, from Woodstock, Ontario, has had plenty of experience. Sometimes the parts he plays are so different from his everyday life that special preparations are necessary. To get into character for some of his roles, Kevin has learned to speak with an accent, worn an uncomfortable leg brace, pretended to be physically and mentally challenged and suffered through a horrible hairdo. For one episode of "The X-Files," he was even rigged with some bloody special effects.

Kevin Zegers

Photos: Courtesy of Mary Ellen Zegers

Luna Balloons

by Nick Sullivan

Professor Pirogi and Dave and Miranda
　　Were sitting one morning out on the verandah,
Sitting and sipping their juice in the sun,
　　Talking together of things they had done.

Professor Pirogi had been on the sea
　　In a big wooden boat to a place called Paree.
Miranda had travelled alone on a train;
　　She'd gone to the mountains and come back again.
For Pirogi was bold and Miranda was brave,
　　But no one was bolder and braver than Dave:
"I went on a trip in a yellow balloon,"
　　Said he, "till at last I came down on the moon!"

"But that cannot be!" the professor replied.
　　"The moon is so hot that you would have been fried!
Or else it's so cold that you would have been frozen
　　Like ice in an ice-box. But even supposin'
You'd gone, as you say, in a yellow balloon
　　Way up in the sky and come down on the moon,
You'd quickly discover it's airless and bleak.
　　Why, even a mouse could not live there a week!
And if you went walking, then sooner or later
　　You'd trip on a rock and fall into a crater,
For everyone knows, if they look at the facts,
　　That craters and crevices, crannies and cracks
Are common up there as are fish in the sea,
　　As pigs in a puddle, or leaves on a tree."

31

"So pretend, if you will, that a bed is a chair,
 That horses can whistle, that one is a pair,
That water is dry and that mirrors have hair,
 That chickens play chess at the top of the stair,
That nothing tastes worse than a chocolate eclair;
 Pretend what you want to pretend — I don't care!
That wombats eat worms with a fork and a spoon —
 But do not pretend you have been to the moon!"

"But listen, professor," said Dave, in the end,
 "I'm telling the truth — I don't need to pretend.
You say that the moon is both airless and grey,
 Too hot or too cold and too far, far away.
But these are just things you have read in a book.
 You'd know they were wrong if you'd been there to look!"

"For I flew my yellow balloon to the skies
 And I saw the moon with my very own eyes:
I saw purple people all wearing bow ties
 Who live upon nothing but blueberry pies,
While shadowy things of incredible size
 Flit softly and swiftly like black butterflies
And sit on a person they hear telling lies
 And do not allow him or her to arise
Regardless of struggles or pitiful cries
 Until that poor person decides to be wise
 And promises never again to tell lies."

"And that's what you'd see if you went to the moon,
 As I went there once in my yellow balloon!"

"Well, well!" said Professor Pirogi, "Well, well!
　　In all of my books I have never heard tell
Of any of this. It just goes to show
　　There's things even those who write books do not know!"

"It sounds most exciting!" Miranda agreed,
　　"Much more exciting than something you'd read!
Although we are bold and although we are brave,
　　There's nobody braver or bolder than Dave!
But do tell us more of your trip to the moon,
　　The trip that you made in your yellow balloon!"

"You could hardly believe all the things I saw there!"
　　Said Dave, "Like the houses that float in the air,
And elephants dancing a waltz cheek to cheek;
　　If I told you it all it would take me a week!
And if —" But then Dave turned around in surprise,
　　For the rustle of wings could be heard in the skies
As three shadowy things of incredible size
　　Came softy and swiftly like black butterflies
And sat upon Dave for telling his lies.
　　And they did not allow him to stir or arise,
Ignoring his struggles and pitiful cries
　　Until he decided at last to be wise
And never again to be heard telling lies
　　About trips he had made in a yellow balloon —
And then they flew back to the moon.

Illustrations by Patrick Fitzgerald

Somewhere in your Mind

by Susan Petersiel Berg

Did you know you can take a trip without ever leaving home? Try using your imagination.

That's what hundreds of writers, film-makers and animators do to create wonderful worlds to share with you. Fasten your seatbelt — it's going to be a wondrous ride!

Over the Rainbow

If you've heard a munchkin sing or seen a yellow brick road, you probably have some idea about Oz. Oz was created by L. Frank Baum, author of *The Wonderful Wizard of Oz* and other Oz books.

Oz is shaped like a rectangle. In the very centre is the capital, Emerald City. The people who live in Oz are munchkins — full-grown, they are the size of a 10-year-old. Although the people live in four separate countries, they all obey the ruler of Oz, Princess Ozma.

How do you get to Oz? Well, that's a bit tricky. The country is surrounded by sand on all sides, and anyone who steps on the sand turns to dust. So the only way to get to Oz is by flying in, as Dorothy did. Even that presents a problem. Because Princess Ozma decided her country should be invisible, you can't see where it is when you fly over it!

IMPASSABLE DESERT

Winged
Monkeys

Sapphire
City

GILLIKIN COUNTRY

Lake
Orizon

Munchkin
Mountains

WINKIE
COUNTRY

MUNCHKIN
COUNTRY

Bottle Hill

The
Woodman
Castle

Poppy
Field

DEADLY DESERT

First
Yellow
Brick Road

Where Dorothy's
House Landed

SHIFTING SANDS

Scarecrow
Tower

Fiddlestick
Forest

EMERALD
CITY
Lake Quad

Crystal
City

Crystal
Mountains

QUADLING
COUNTRY

Glinda's Palace

GREAT
SANDY WASTE

THE MARVELLOUS *Land of Oz*

The Creation Song

Can you imagine a land that came into being because a lion started singing? That's how the land of Narnia began. It's the setting for *The Narnia Chronicles*, by C.S. Lewis.

Aslan was a great lion from a country beyond the end of the world. He had an amazing voice, and his song was so beautiful that it made things appear from nowhere — stars, planets, the sun, the valley of Narnia, grass, trees, animals, the wild people of the woods.

Visitors to Narnia should take a trip to Aslan's How. It's a maze of tunnels, galleries and caves. The walls of the tunnels are covered with strange characters. Some of the most important parts of Narnia's history are linked to this place, so it's the perfect starting point for a journey.

Who's There?

Who-ville is not only an imaginary place. It's also a really *small* place. It's so small that the whole town fits on a speck of dust. Who-ville was created by Dr. Seuss for the book *Horton Hears a Who*. Other than its size, Who-ville is a regular city — there are houses and schools, lots of people, apartment buildings and more. There's also a town square. It's surrounded by wildly curving walls, with a fountain in the centre. The highest place in Who-ville is the Eiffelberg Tower. Remember though, it's only tall in Who-ville!

TOWN SQUARE
Who-ville

Illustrations by June Bradford

The Trip of a Lifetime

When you're in Miss Frizzle's class, you get to explore a lot of different worlds. But it's not the worlds that are imaginary — it's how you get there. Miss Frizzle is the teacher whose class travels on The Magic Schoolbus in books and on television.

The kids in the class take great field trips. They go undersea, into space, even into the human body. They travel on an old schoolbus. There are all kinds of buttons and levers on the dashboard, and Miss Frizzle is always hitting one of them by accident. When she does — *whoosh!* — both bus and kids shrink. The bus changes shape and becomes some other object. And the kids are off on another amazing adventure!

Da Vinci's Vision

by Fareena Kanhai

*I*talian artist Leonardo da Vinci constantly used his imagination. From his head and his pencil came hundreds of ideas for inventions. The only problem with them was that they were way ahead of their time.

After a while, his notebooks were hidden — or lost — and so were his great ideas. It was hundreds of years before other inventors would create what Leonardo dreamed of in the 1400s.

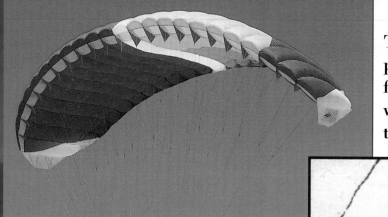

Today skydivers use parachutes like this one. The first successful parachute jump was made from the top of a tower in France in 1783.

In 1485, Leonardo sketched this parachute. He even noted what size it would have to be so that the wearer could fall safely from a great height.

Thanks to Jacques-Yves Cousteau and Emile Gagnon, SCUBA divers can swim underwater without any connection to the surface. They breathe compressed air from tanks on their backs. These tanks were invented by Cousteau and Gagnon in 1943.

Leonardo imagined the same possibility — swimming underwater without a hose to connect the swimmer to the surface. This drawing shows his idea of a crush-proof air chamber attached to the diver's chest.

Helicopters don't require long runways because they take off straight up and land straight down. The first helicopter that could carry a person was designed and flown by Paul Cornu in 1907.

This flying machine is one of many that Leonardo designed. He imagined that a rotating air screw would move it through the sky.

This airplane has its landing gear down. Once it's in the air, the landing gear folds up to make the plane more streamlined and efficient. The first airplane with landing gear that could fold away was built in 1933.

Leonardo never saw his flying machines fly. But he knew it was important that they have landing gear that pulled up and could be let down.

Wonders of SCIENCE

by Melvin Berger

We can create all kinds of wonderful places just by using our imaginations. But there's another place that's full of wonder — the world of science.

Can you pass through a door without opening it? Hardly! But sound waves can. Say you're on the outside of a metal door. *Crash!* Someone drops something inside the room. You can hear it, even though you're not in the room. That's because a dropped object makes the air around it vibrate. The vibrations form a sound wave in the air. The sound wave travels through the air — and through the metal door — to your ear.

WOW!

Sound travels through the air at 1190 km/h. The Concorde flies nearly twice that fast, at over 2300 km/h. A space shuttle gets to around 25 000 km/h!

I magine something so strong that it can cut diamonds, but so exact that it can be used for surgery. Sound impossible? It's not — it's a laser beam.

A laser beam is a very powerful beam of light. Light beams are made up of tiny particles called photons. In regular light beams, the photons are scattered around. But in laser beams, the photons all travel together, making a much stronger beam. So what can a laser do? It can cut fabric, weld metal, cut and seal blood vessels — and play the CD on your CD player.

The light of some lasers is 1000 times brighter than the sun!

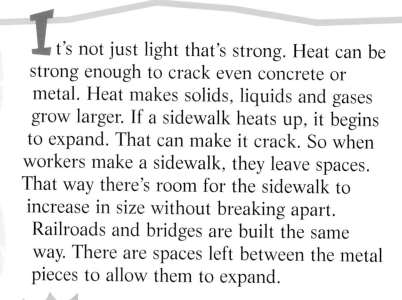

It's not just light that's strong. Heat can be strong enough to crack even concrete or metal. Heat makes solids, liquids and gases grow larger. If a sidewalk heats up, it begins to expand. That can make it crack. So when workers make a sidewalk, they leave spaces. That way there's room for the sidewalk to increase in size without breaking apart. Railroads and bridges are built the same way. There are spaces left between the metal pieces to allow them to expand.

Illustrations by Janet McLeod

WOW! The hottest place on Earth is Libya. The temperature can reach 136.4° C in the shade.

Like sound, air can really move! When warm and cold air meet, the cold air pushes the warm air up. The sun warms air unevenly. The air gets very hot in places. Then it rises and cool air rushes in to take its place. All that moving air is what we call wind. When strong winds start to blow, there can be trouble. Hurricanes blow at speeds of more than 120 km/h. The winds in tornadoes blow even faster — up to 400 km/h. But tornado winds follow a very narrow path and last only a short time, so they do less damage than hurricanes.

WOW!

Air presses on your body with a weight of about 15 tonnes!

How to Tell a Story

People are born storytellers. Even very young children tell stories about the things that happen to them.

In ancient times, people had no books. They passed their stories by word of mouth from person to person and generation to generation. Many of those stories still exist today.

In this magazine, you met storyteller Louise Profit-Leblanc. You also read *Luna Balloona*, which is a tall tale, and *Boy Soup*, which is a fantasy. These are two kinds of stories that are often told rather than written. Others include fairy tales, myths, legends — and dinner-table anecdotes.

People like telling stories, but they like hearing them too. That's why a lot of people like Louise Profit-Leblanc make a career, or a hobby, of telling stories. They make stories come alive, sometimes simply by changing the sound of their voices, or by wearing costumes, using props, singing or speaking in rhyme.

Telling a story well takes a bit of effort. But it's fun! Here's your chance to choose a story and tell it to a group of people.

45

1. Write Your Script

Choose a story you'd like to tell, or retell, to others. It could be a well-known fairy tale or a legend. It could be *Luna Balloona* or *Boy Soup*, or another story you've read. It could even be an experience from your own life. The library and the Internet are both good places to find stories.

Create a script to help you learn your story. Your script should be organized so it helps you tell the story. Some storytellers like to work just from an outline. They list the major events on paper, then fill in the details as they speak. Others like to write down the whole story, using their own words. Keep your first draft short — about one or two pages.

2. Plan Your Delivery

Look over your script. How do you want your audience to feel when they hear your story? Is the story happy or sad, funny or scary? You'll want to create the right mood for your audience. There are lots of ways to do that. Think about:

- using hand and body movements
- using sound effects
- using different voices
- using recorded music or an instrument
- using props
- using costumes

Decide what you'd like to add to your story. Using your first draft, write directions to yourself about what you want to add. This will help you to remember where you want to use a prop, have a sound effect, add movement and so on.

If You Are Using a Computer . . .

Input your first draft on the computer. You will find it easy to add and change anything you wish to change as you work on your final draft.

3. Practise Your Story

Practise telling your story. The first few times, use your script or outline. It will help you remember the details so you get the story right. It will also help you figure out exactly when the gestures, props, music or sound effects should come into the story. As soon as you can, practise without looking at what you wrote. Tell your story in front of a mirror so you can watch your movements. Tell it to a friend or a member of your family and ask for suggestions. Eventually you'll be able to tell the story from memory, using all the special effects and props you've planned.

How Am I Doing?

Before you step in front of your audience, take a minute to ask yourself these questions:

- Do I know my story well enough?
- Do I know where I want people to laugh, cry, be scared and so on?
- Do I have my props ready and laid out for easy use?

Tip

You might want to tape record your special effects. Ask a helper to play the tape for you while you're telling your story. Give him or her a script that shows when the tape should be played.

4. Tell Your Story

When you're happy with the way you tell the story, present it to an audience. You can tell it to your classmates, a group of neighbours or some of your friends. If your story is suitable for young children, you might ask if you can tell it to a grade one or two class.

You can tell if you've done a good job by watching how interested your audience is. But you can also ask for suggestions for making your story better. And you can learn from other storytellers. Whenever you hear someone else tell a story, think about what you like or don't like about the presentation. What ideas could you use the next time you tell a story?

Illustrations by Claudia Dávila